Bond
Reasoning Puzzles

9-12 years

Lynn Adams

Verbal Reasoning

Nelson Thornes

Who's Right?

Four friends, Abna, Beth, Colette and Denzel, were going to see a Saturday showing of an action film. When they got to the cinema they saw this poster:

On reading the poster, each child thought something different.

Abna thought:

… the film will definitely last for one and a half hours.

Beth thought:

… Denzel wouldn't be able to see the film as he wasn't going to be 13 until next month.

Colette thought:

… that they would have to come back later as the film wouldn't start until after lunch.

Denzel thought:

… that they could use the family ticket to save some money.

Who was right? _____

Before and After

Can you find the missing word that, when added to the given words, makes two new words? To help you get started, the first one has been completed.

1 sun __light__
  __light__ house

7 week ____/____
  _____ less

2
  jelly ____/____
  _____ cake

8
  wild ____ life ____
  ____ life ____ boat

3 butter _____
  _____ cake

9 work ____/____
  _____ case

4
  sauce ____/____
  _____ cake

10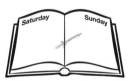
  milk ____/____
  _____ kind

5 news _____/____
  ____/____ weight

11 post _____/____
  _____ board

6
  tooth ____/____
  _____ pocket

12
  eye _____
  _____ point

HINT The drawings will give you some clues as to the missing words.

Sign Language

In British sign language each letter of the alphabet has a special hand sign. Can you use the hand signs shown in the key below to work out what each word means?

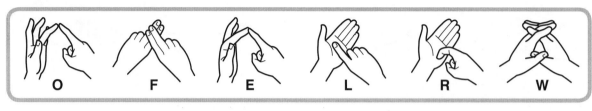

A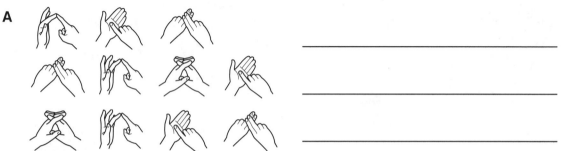

_____

_____

_____

B   The six signed letters in the key form one six-letter word. Can you unscramble the letters to find the word?

_____

C   There are several other words (made up of 2–5 letters) that can be made using these six signed letters. How many can you find?

_____ _____ _____ _____

_____ _____ _____ _____

_____ _____ _____ _____

_____ _____ _____ _____

_____ _____

Hidden Creatures

Can you find one of these creatures hidden between two words in each of the sentences below? The first one has been found for you.

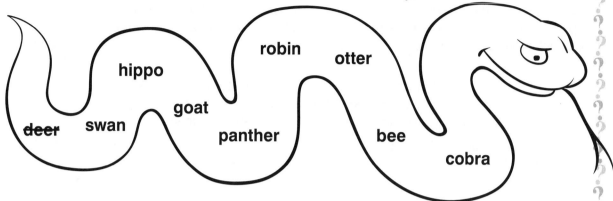

robin   otter   hippo   goat   ~~deer~~   swan   panther   bee   cobra

1   Mr Rena<u>de er</u>ased the homework from the board before I had a chance to copy it down.

2   At the film premiere, the girls began screaming as the teenage heart-throb invited them to step under the rope barrier.

3   My grandparents are learning the tango at the community centre in their village.

4   The audience gasped as the magician's wand flew out of his hand and landed in the lap of a lady in the front row.

5   Jacob ran all the way home to tell his mum that he'd made it on to the hockey team.

6   At the dinner table, my mother became cross as she reminded my sister that it's not terribly polite to chew with your mouth open.

7   In my comic book, the flippant hero smiled and waved at the crowd as he lifted the car with one hand to rescue the damsel in distress.

8   The guns that fired from the battleship pounded the enemy as they ran to hide in caves along the coast.

9   Martin hated the party so much that he stayed hidden in the wardrobe even after the other children had left.

10 My four-year-old cousin drew a picture for me of a peanut wearing a hat and striped scarf.

> **HINT**
> Beware! The last sentence includes a creature that isn't on the list.

The missing animal is _____!

It's Your Go!

Jack, Jill and Humpty Dumpty are playing different versions of the same card game. The point of the game is to find the card that keeps the pattern going. Look at the cards that have already been played in each game to spot the pattern. Then decide which card should be played next and write or draw it on the empty card.

HINT Be sure to think about both the number of the card as well as its suit (hearts ♡, spades ♠, clubs ♣ or diamonds ◇). In a pack of cards, the cards go up in order, from lowest to highest, like this:

| Ace | 2 | 3 | 4 | 5 | 6 | 7 | 8 | 9 | 10 | Jack | Queen | King |

Which card should Jack play next?

Which card should Jill play next?

Humpty Dumpty gets an extra go. Which two cards should he play?

followed by

Build the Wall

Lorenzo has to repair a wall by the end of the day. So far he has placed two of the remaining bricks in the wall but eight bricks are still missing. Can you help him finish it so he can go home on time?

The wall is made up of bricks and each brick has a word label. To place the right brick in each gap, you must find the brick that has a label that means the same as the bricks directly above or below it. We've done two for you.

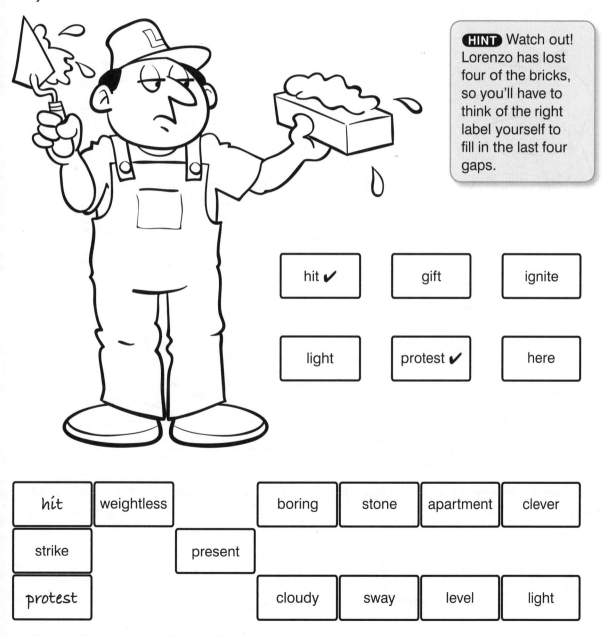

HINT Watch out! Lorenzo has lost four of the bricks, so you'll have to think of the right label yourself to fill in the last four gaps.

| hit ✔ | gift | ignite |
| light | protest ✔ | here |

hit	weightless		boring	stone	apartment	clever
strike		present				
protest			cloudy	sway	level	light

Fish Ponds

Yesterday, Alison's Aquatics delivered 10 new fish to the local garden centre. George, the owner of the garden centre, wasn't working then and has arrived this morning to find that some of the fish have been put into the wrong ponds.

Only similar types of fish can be kept together, so he needs to remove the new fish straightaway and transfer them into their own ponds. Can you help George identify the two new fish in each pond that don't belong by drawing a circle around them?

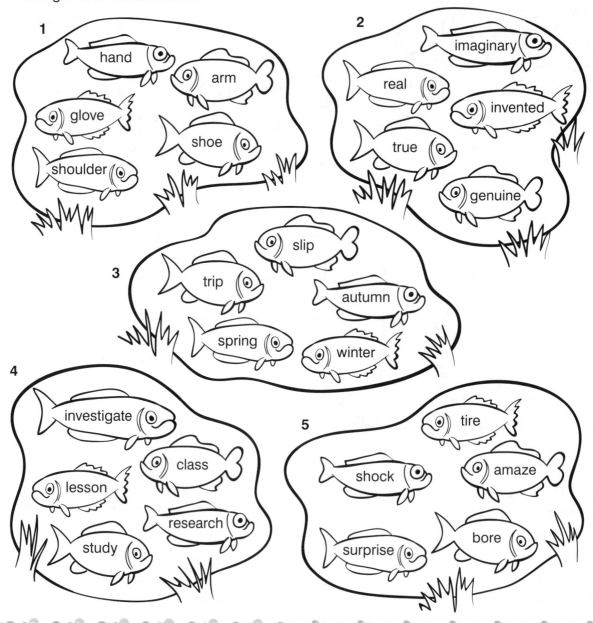

1

hand
arm
glove
shoe
shoulder

2

imaginary
real
invented
true
genuine

3

slip
trip
autumn
spring
winter

4

investigate
class
lesson
research
study

5

tire
shock
amaze
surprise
bore

Roll of the Dice

Five friends are in the middle of playing a game of chance. After the first round, Nathan must total their scores to work out who will be going through to the final. Only the top two scores will go through. Using the game dice shown below, help Nathan to complete the scorecard.

| 2 = A | 3 = B | 4 = C | 5 = D | 6 = E |

Name	Roll	Score
Lucy	$(A \times B) + C$	_____
Kate	$(E - D) \times C$	_____
Nathan	$\dfrac{D \times C}{A}$	_____
Ali	$A + B - C + D + E$	_____
Jean-Baptiste	$(B \times B) - (D - A)$	_____

1 Who got the highest score? _____

2 Which two players need to roll again to decide who the second finalist will be?

_____ and _____

At the Cinema

Reese and some of his friends went to the cinema on Saturday afternoon. From the information given below, can you work out where each person sat to watch the film? When you've worked it out, write the name of each person on his or her seat.

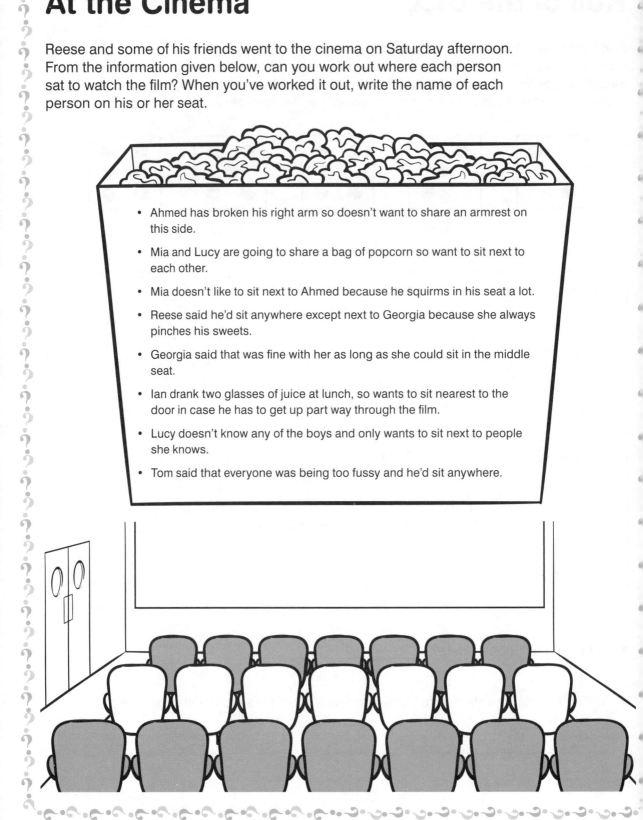

- Ahmed has broken his right arm so doesn't want to share an armrest on this side.
- Mia and Lucy are going to share a bag of popcorn so want to sit next to each other.
- Mia doesn't like to sit next to Ahmed because he squirms in his seat a lot.
- Reese said he'd sit anywhere except next to Georgia because she always pinches his sweets.
- Georgia said that was fine with her as long as she could sit in the middle seat.
- Ian drank two glasses of juice at lunch, so wants to sit nearest to the door in case he has to get up part way through the film.
- Lucy doesn't know any of the boys and only wants to sit next to people she knows.
- Tom said that everyone was being too fussy and he'd sit anywhere.

Dear Planet Earth

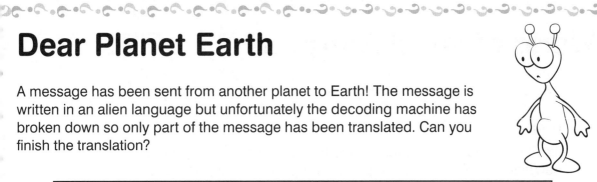

A message has been sent from another planet to Earth! The message is written in an alien language but unfortunately the decoding machine has broken down so only part of the message has been translated. Can you finish the translation?

CONFIDENTIAL

TOP SECRET

```
X f    d p n f    j o    q f b d f.    X f    x b o u
_ _    c _ _ _    _ _    p _ a c _.    _ _    _ a _ _

p o m z    p o f    u i j o h  –  u p    d p n f
_ _ _ _    _ _ _    _ _ _ _ _    _ _    c _ _ _

b o e    x b u d i    b o    F b s u i m j o h
a _ _    _ a _ _ _    a _    _ a _ _ _  _ _ _ _

d s j d l f u    n b u d i.
c _ _ c _ _ _    _ a _ c _.
```

To: Our Alien Friends

From: Your Earthling Friends

We Earthlings need to send back a message to the aliens. Can you translate this message back into the aliens' language?

```
Y o u    a r e    m o s t    w e l c o m e,    f r i e n d s.
_ _ _    _ _ _    _ _ _ _    _ _ _ _ _ _ _,    _ _ _ _ _ _ _.
```

HINT It may help if you write out the alphabet!

World of Word Burgers

Help! World of Word Burgers is having a lunchtime rush and customers are queuing up for their burgers. Grab an apron and help make some word burgers!

To make the burgers, take away one letter from the word that is given to get a new word and write it in the top of the burger bun. Then, add one letter to the given word to get another word and write it in the bottom half of the burger bun. Next to each burger is an order ticket – the ticket has some clues to help you complete each burger. The first one has been done for you.

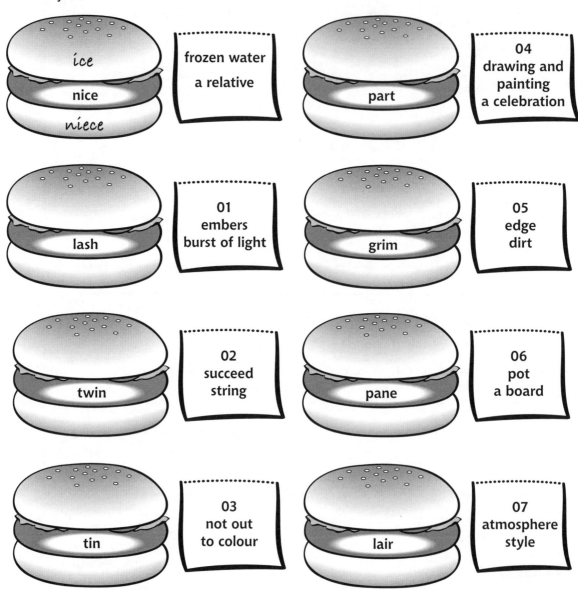

ice
nice
niece

frozen water
a relative

part

04
drawing and
painting
a celebration

lash

01
embers
burst of light

grim

05
edge
dirt

twin

02
succeed
string

pane

06
pot
a board

tin

03
not out
to colour

lair

07
atmosphere
style

Ship Ahoy!

Number World Games needs to ship some boxes to four different countries. They've identified each box with a mathematical label and Danny, the warehouse manager, now has to make sure that the boxes reach the right locations. Can you help Danny match up the right boxes with the right ships at the docks?

HINT Solve the box labels and the ship labels and then match each box with a ship.

1   10 + 10 − 3

2   16 − 5 + 1

3   22 − 20 + 9

4   10 × $\frac{3}{2}$

Ship _____   11 + 8 − 2

Ship _____   3 × 2 + 5

Ship _____ $\frac{9}{3}$ × 4

Ship _____   6 × 2 + 3

Ship _____   10 × 0 + 11

What am I? 1

Can you solve the riddles to answer the questions?

Pass the tissues

My first is in ONCE but never in ONE,

My second's in POUR and also in SOME,

My third is in LONE but never in PHONE,

My fourth is in DOWN but never in KNOWN,

My whole can be caught but can never be thrown!

What am I? _____

Up and down

My first is in HUSH and also in SPARE,

My second's in TEA but never in BEAR,

My third is in PLAY and also in FAIR,

My fourth is in SILLY but never in SALLY,

My fifth is in ROW and also in RALLY,

My sixth is in SPIN and also in RUSTLE,

My whole can climb up without moving a muscle!

What am I? _____

HINT Each line is a clue to a letter of the alphabet – put the letters in order to find the answer to the question.

Here and There

Ruth is going on holiday with her family. She has a long car drive ahead of her so has come up with a game to keep herself busy. She's borrowed her dad's map and is making up abbreviations for the names of some of the towns and counties she sees on the map. Can you help her finish writing the abbreviations? Each abbreviation follows a pattern. Work out the patterns, then write the abbreviations of the places that still need to be done.

1   Buckinghamshire, Bucks   Cambridgeshire, Cambs   Hertfordshire,   _____

2   Stirlingshire, shireS   Roxburghshire, shireR   Perthshire,   _____

3   Dockray, Yard   Eastington, Note   Shaldon,   _____

4   Nettlecombe, Been   Maltongate, Team   Sidmouth,   _____

5   Rackenford, Rack   Tintwistle, Lint   Waterville,   _____

While on holiday, Ruth's dad is going to drive her to a beach to meet her friend Monica but he needs to know the directions. Monica loves puzzles, so has written some of the directions in code. Can you help Ruth work out the code and complete the directions?

So, remember that north, south, east and west are:
6531X   47Z1   84Z1   Z521X.

But which is which?!

Head 84Z1 _____ for six miles then go Z521X _____ until the roundabout. Take the first right, then head 6531X _____ on the motorway for two miles. Take the exit, turn 47Z1 _____ and you'll be in 13235 _____. Can't wait to see you!!

> **HINT** You will need to read Monica's hint at the top of the note to start with!

Is Something Out There?

What's going on in Gloxwell? The mystery has left residents rattled, including the newspaper reporter who has written about it. As the newspaper editor, you need to fix the mistakes in the article before the newspaper goes to press. It seems that parts of some words in the text have been left out. You've found the missing groups of letters on the reporter's desk and must now fit them into the correct words to make sure the article makes sense.

HINT Make sure you write the correct words above the mistakes so the reporter will know which words to change!

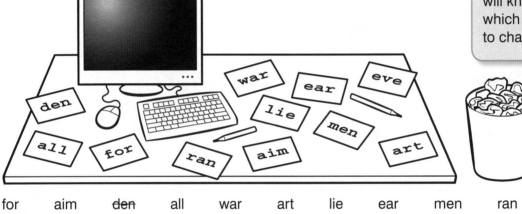

for   aim   ~~den~~   all   war   art   lie   ear   men   ran   eve

Residents

~~Resits~~ of Gloxwell were in a panic last night as bright oge lights lit up the sky. "I've never seen anything like it," cled long-time resident, Pete Wilson. "They weren't like any lights I've ever seen. They weren't planes or weather boons – I don't care what the governt says. They sure weren't from planet Eh."

The lights hovered over Gloxwell for almost an hour bee speeding off tods London.

Not everyone in Gloxwell was concerned. "It's like we're in the middle of a Doctor Who episode. Cool!" said eln-year-old Simon Crumb. "If it's ans, then I hope they abduct me," agreed his friend, Nick Good.

Several people have reported that their cats haven't been seen since the lights apped.

Your Turn!

Gran is teaching James some card games. Today, she is showing him three different games. James hasn't really been paying very much attention and now it's his turn. Can you help him choose which cards to play?

In each of the games, the shown cards all follow a different pattern. Work out the pattern of the cards that are showing and decide which card or cards Ian should play.

> **HINT** Remember, in a pack of cards, the cards go up in order, from lowest to highest, like this:
>
> Ace   2   3   4   5   6   7   8   9   10   Jack   Queen   King

Game 1

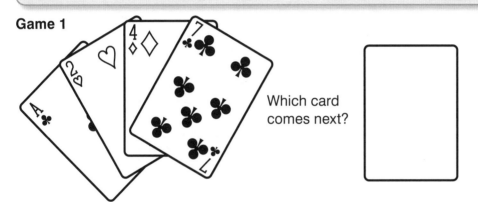

Which card comes next?

Game 2   Write or draw the missing cards in the pattern.

Game 3

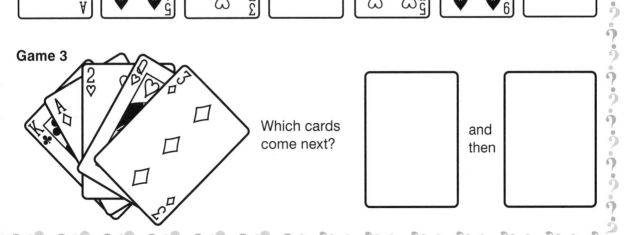

Which cards come next?

and then

Word Soup

Each word in the first soup pot can be added to a word in the second pot to make a new word. Can you create ten new words from the smaller words in the two pots?

HINT The words in the first soup pot don't have to come first in your new words.

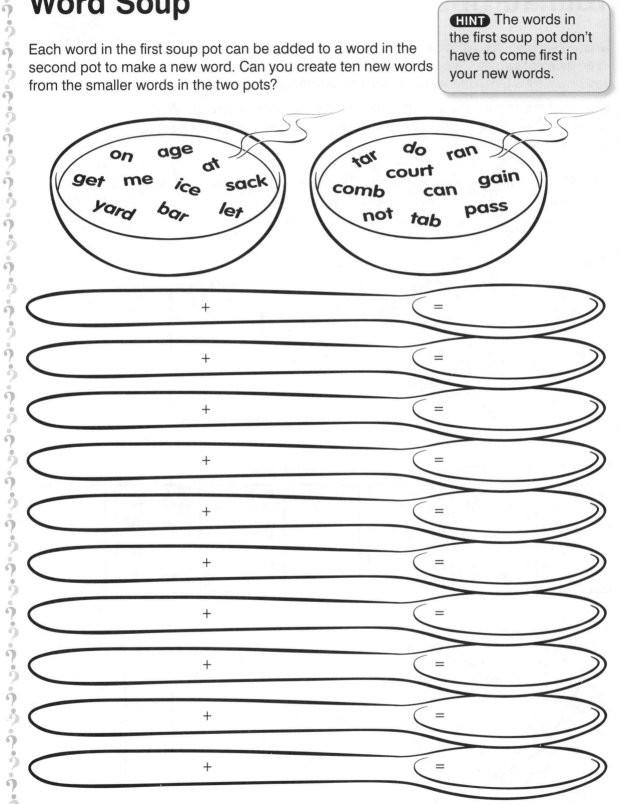

First pot: on age get me at ice sack yard bar let

Second pot: tar do ran court comb can gain not tab pass

+ =

+ =

+ =

+ =

+ =

+ =

+ =

+ =

+ =

+ =

Get Me Out of Here!

A famous actress wants to get out of the jungle but needs to cross the broken word bridge to do it. Help repair the word bridge by writing in the correct missing letter in each empty space. Each letter must finish the word in front of the blank space and begin the word after it. Here's how it works:

w i n d o <u>w</u> a s h i n g

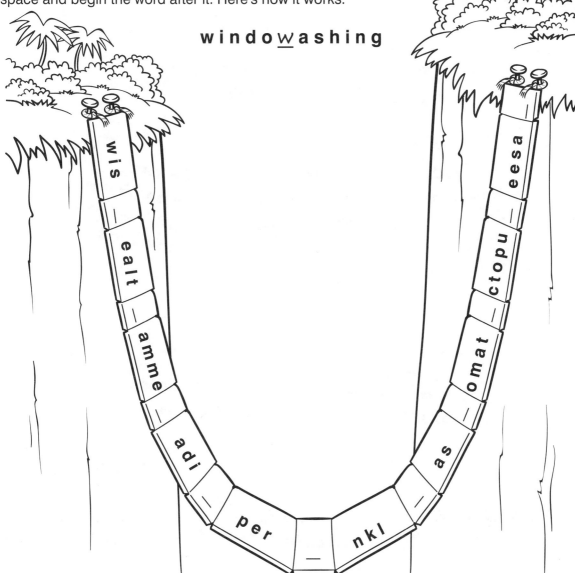

Unscramble the letters you added to find out what the actress looked forward to most when she got out of the jungle.

____ ____ ____ ____ ____ ____ ____ ____ ____!

True or False?

For a school project, Alisha Mann is writing a report about her family's pet cat called Tigs. She has collected some facts about Tigs, which she's written on note cards. There's some other information about Tigs, but only one piece of it is definitely true. Using the information on the note cards, can you work out which other fact about Tigs **must** be true?

Tigs is an orange and white cat.

We adopted Tigs in May.

My eleventh birthday was 2nd May.

Tigs goes to bed and sleeps with me every evening.

Tigs spends most of his time lying in the sun in the garden.

Tigs was given his name because he looks like a tiger.

Tigs was a birthday present for me.

Tigs is my family's only pet.

I play with Tigs in the garden.

Tigs is indoors at night.

HINT Some of the statements **might** be true, but only one is **definitely** true.

Terrible Toddlers!

The town's toddler group meets at the library every Wednesday. Today, the little ones have had a great time but, unfortunately, that included wandering around the library and pulling books off the shelves to use as building blocks! In this library the books are not necessarily ordered alphabetically, so help the librarians reshelve the books by working out where each book belongs.

Use the first letter of each word in the book title to work out the pattern. Then find the book on the trolley that continues that pattern and write its name in the correct space on the shelf. But be warned, not all of the books on the trolley fit on these shelves!

HINT Don't count the '&' signs!

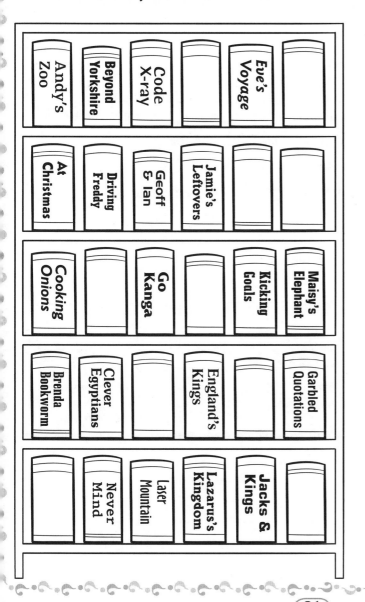

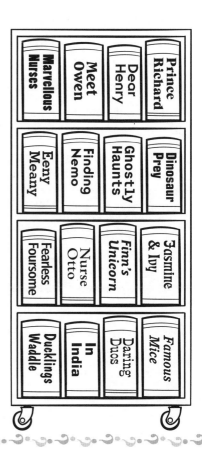

Brain Benders

A The Seven Dwarfs have been asked to open their village fete. Unfortunately, the villagers can't remember which dwarf is which, so they've asked some of their children to write down the clothes each of the dwarfs usually wears. The children have done a good job, except they can't remember what colour top Doc wears. Can you help?

Sleepy is always taking Dopey's shirt by mistake because it looks like his.

Grumpy has a long beard and wears a red top.

Bashful has a long beard like Grumpy but wears a brown top like Happy and Sneezy.

Dopey wears a purple hat and a green top.

Each of the Seven Dwarfs wears the same colour top as at least one of the other dwarfs.

What colour top does Doc wear? _____

B The school drama club has ordered some individual pizzas to celebrate the first performance of the school play. Can you work out which person gets which pizza?

Martin won't eat any vegetables, only meat, and likes lots of toppings.

Anna is a vegetarian but doesn't like mushrooms.

Mandy likes her pizza full of toppings, at least three, and likes a mixture of meat and vegetables.

Manuel doesn't like meat or green food.

Rolf will only eat pizza that has one of each type of food on it (one type of meat, one type of vegetable).

Mr Wilson likes only pepperoni or ham, but not both together. He also doesn't like pineapple or onion.

Type of Pizza / Person	Three-meat special: pepperoni, ham and sausage	Pepperoni	Red pepper, tomato and mushroom	Ham and onion	Tomato, basil and olive	Pineapple, basil, tomato and sausage
Martin						
Anna						
Mandy						
Manuel						
Rolf						
Mr Wilson						

Find the Missing Letters

Here are some code webs. Can you break each code and fill in the missing letters? Work out the code in the web on the left. Then use it to find the answer to the web on the right.

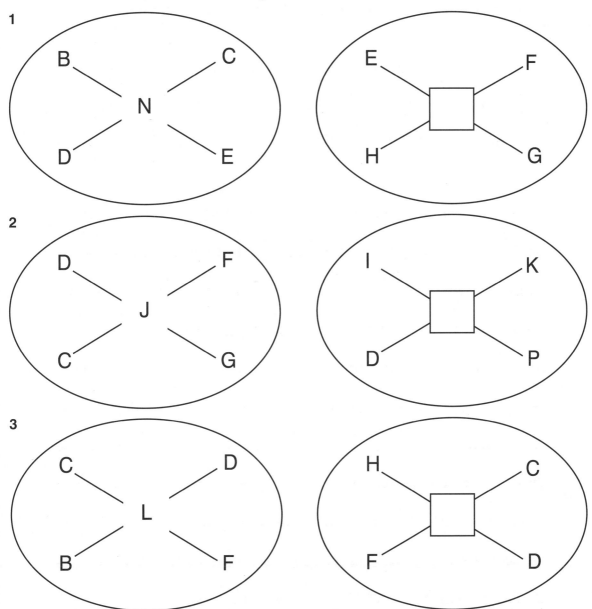

1

B   C
N
D   E

E   F
☐
H   G

2

D   F
J
C   G

I   K
☐
D   P

3

C   D
L
B   F

H   C
☐
F   D

HINT You will need to use your maths skills (adding, subtracting, dividing or multiplying). A–Z = 1–26. Each letter may be used only once. If you get stuck, try using the top letters and bottom letters separately.

It's a Mystery!

Darcy Danger is writing a mystery story, but is having trouble coming up with the right words. She's written the first paragraph, but isn't happy with some of the words she's used. Help Darcy improve her story by finding the word that means the same as the underlined word and writing the new word above it.

wearily	drifting	remembered	seized
stormy	back	insane	endure	noted
withhold	convict	dangerous	perceived	roused

It was a dark and <u>unsettled</u> night. Doris Darling turned over in bed, pulling the covers up to her chin. She could <u>withstand</u> the weather as long as she was warm and cosy in bed. As she was <u>floating</u> off to sleep, Doris began to dream about a <u>hazardous</u> <u>criminal</u> who had escaped from a prison for the criminally <u>mad</u>. Just as the police put the man in handcuffs, Doris was <u>woken</u> from her sleep to hear Mr Pips, her cat, softly tapping on the <u>rear</u> door to be let in. Tap, tap, tap. Tap, tap, tap. <u>Tiredly</u>, Doris climbed out of bed and padded her way across the room, down the stairs and through the kitchen to the door. Just as her hand released the lock, panic <u>grabbed</u> her as she <u>recalled</u> that she hadn't let Mr Pips out that night. Who or what was out there?

HINT Beware! Not all of the words on Darcy's list will be needed.

House!

Sammy, Jules and Josie are playing a game of number sentence bingo. They each have three numbers left to cross off their cards before they can get a full house. Can you solve the bingo caller's next six calls to find out who will be the first to call 'House!' and win the jackpot? Write the winner's name in the congratulations star.

Call 1: $7 \times 6 - 5 = 3 \times 4 + ($ _____ $)$

Call 2: $\frac{36}{6} + 4 = ($ _____ $) - 3 + 4$

Call 3: $\frac{21}{7} + 10 = \frac{24}{4} + ($ _____ $)$

Call 4: $3^2 \times 11 - 34 = 10 \times 8 - ($ _____ $)$

Call 5: $14 \times 2 + 6 = 8 \times 4 + ($ _____ $)$

Call 6: $\frac{30}{2} + 5 = 16 \times 2 - ($ _____ $)$

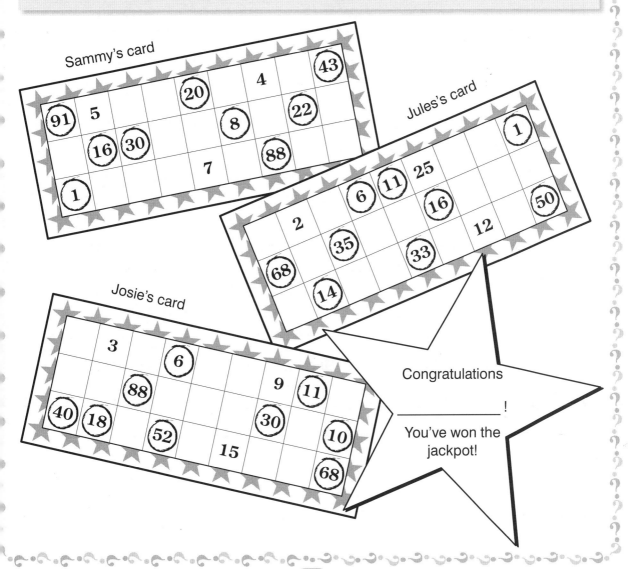

Sammy's card

Jules's card

Josie's card

Congratulations

_____ !

You've won the jackpot!

Alice in Wonderland

While playing in her grandmother's attic room, Tessa found a dusty scroll at the bottom of a bookcase. As she unravelled it, she saw that it was a handwritten section of a story. When she showed it to her grandma, she laughed, and said that it was a page from the 'opposite' tale of *Alice in Wonderland* that she had started writing many years ago.

Tessa then went to find her own copy of the story, so that she could see the changes Grandma had made in her version. Tessa underlined 10 words that Grandma had swapped for their opposites in this section of the story. Using the group of original words at the top of the scroll and Tessa's underlined words, can you work out where each original word would have been placed? Write the original words at the bottom of the page.

old	startled	affectionately	stingy	pleasant
sour	savage	forgotten	hopeful	perhaps

"You can't think how glad I am to see you again, you dear <u>young</u>[1] thing!" said the Duchess, as she tucked her arm <u>coldly</u>[2] into Alice's, and they walked off together. Alice was very glad to find her in such a <u>disagreeable</u>[3] temper, and thought to herself that <u>definitely</u>[4] it was only the pepper that had made her so <u>tame</u>[5] when they met in the kitchen.

"When I'm a Duchess," she said to herself, (not in a very <u>pessimistic</u>[6] tone though), "I won't have any pepper in my kitchen at all. Soup does very well without. Maybe it's always pepper that makes people hot-tempered," she went on, very much pleased at having found out a new kind of rule, "and vinegar that makes them <u>sweet</u>[7] – and camomile that makes them bitter – and – and barley-sugar and such things that make children sweet-tempered. I only wish people knew that: then they wouldn't be so <u>generous</u>[8] about it, you know –"

She had quite <u>remembered</u>[9] the Duchess by this time, and was a little <u>calmed</u>[10] when she heard her voice close to her ear. "You're thinking about something, my dear, and that makes you forget to talk."

1 _____ 2 _____ 3 _____ 4 _____

5 _____ 6 _____ 7 _____ 8 _____

9 _____ 10 _____

It's a Lot of Hot Air!

It's time for the annual hot air balloon race again! This year, the balloons are going to be powered by pairs of words. The two words in a word pair relate to each other in some way. As a pilot's helper on race day, it's your job to work out how the words in each word pair are connected. When you've found the link for each pair, write it next to the balloon. The participants are lining up, so let's get started.

HINT The three word pairs on each balloon have the same type of link!

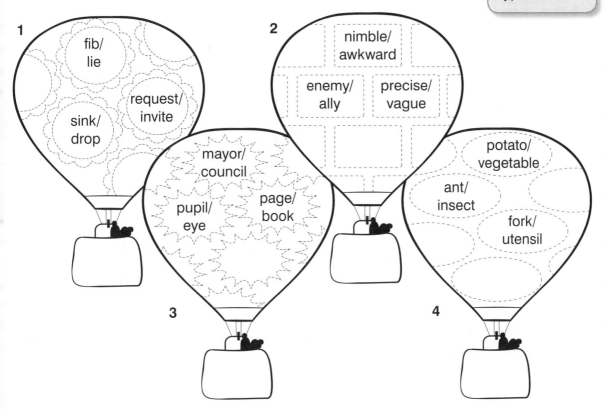

1.
- fib/ lie
- request/ invite
- sink/ drop

2.
- nimble/ awkward
- enemy/ ally
- precise/ vague

3.
- mayor/ council
- pupil/ eye
- page/ book

4.
- potato/ vegetable
- ant/ insect
- fork/ utensil

The balloons will need a good deal of power to get going, so they'll need fuelling with more word pairs. Can you work out which balloon each word pair will fuel?
Write the balloon's number below each word pair.

orang-utan/ mammal	unite/ divide	suspend/ hang	peril/ safety	banish/ remove	handle/ hammer
————	————	————	————	————	————

cheddar/ cheese	pip/ orange	cunning/ crafty	encyclopaedia/ book	mother/ family	release/ hold
————	————	————	————	————	————

Can You Crack the Code?

Shane has started to work out the coded message below but has got stuck. Can you finish off decoding the message for him?

> **HINT** Use this alphabet line to help you.
>
> A B C D E F G H I J K L M N O P Q R S T U V W X Y Z

Gsv givzhfiv xsvhg xzm yv ulfmw mvcg
_ _ _   _ _ _ a _ u _ _   _ _ _ _ _   _ _ _   _ _   _ o u _   _   _ _ _ _

gl gsv xlxlmfg givv, fmwvi gsv yozxp
_ o   _ _ _   _ o _ o _ u _   _ _ _ _,   u _ _ _   _ _ _   _ _ _ _

ilxp. Yfg yvdziv, gsv xsvhg nzb mlg yv
_ _ _ .   _ _ _   _ _ _ _ _ ,   _ _ _   _ _ _ _ _   _ _ _   _ _ _   _ _

gsvlmob gsrmt srwwvm fmwvi gsv ilxp!
_ _ _ _ _ _ _   _ _ _ _ _   _ _ _ _ _ _   _ _ _ _ _   _ _ _   _ _ _ _ !

Now encode this reply! In this code each letter of the alphabet becomes a number; starting with A = 26 and ending with Z = 1.

Aye aye, Captain Smith. Found the
_ _ _   _ _ _,   _ _ _ _ _ _ _   _ _ _ _ _.   _ _ _ _ _   _ _ _

rock, but it looks like your old
_ _ _ _ ,   _ _ _   _ _   _ _ _ _ _   _ _ _ _   _ _ _ _   _ _ _

enemy Peg Leg got there first!
_ _ _ _ _   _ _ _   _ _ _   _ _ _   _ _ _ _ _   _ _ _ _ _ !

My Shopping Basket

Help! I've dropped my shopping basket and everything has fallen onto the floor. One of the shop assistants is helping me pick up my shopping and he has noticed that the barcode labels have been ripped off some of the items. I need to put the right barcode on each food item or I won't be able to buy them – can you help?

Here's what I had in my basket, plus the missing barcode labels.

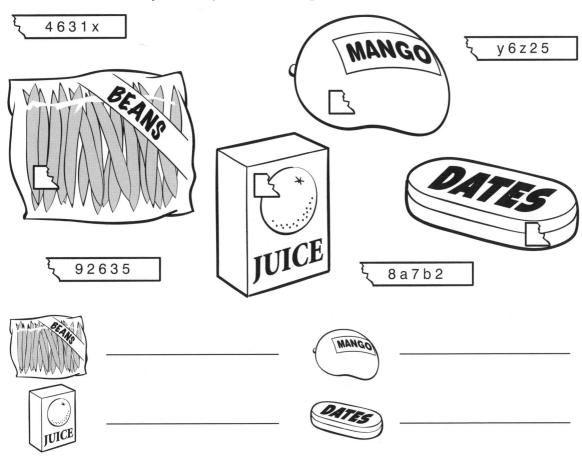

4 6 3 1 x

y 6 z 2 5

9 2 6 3 5

8 a 7 b 2

BEANS _____   MANGO _____

JUICE _____   DATES _____

I've just reached the discount shelf and have found some pre-packed foods that have lost their description labels. In case there is something here that I want, I've decided to take each packet to the barcode reader to find out what's in each one.
What do you think the barcode reader will say that each packet contains?

3 a z 5 _____   b x b x 6 _____

x 3 7 x 3 5 _____   z x 4 6 z x 2 5 _____

What am I? 2

Can you solve the riddles and answer the questions?

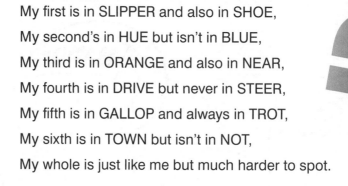

Look, quick!

My first is in SLIPPER and also in SHOE,

My second's in HUE but isn't in BLUE,

My third is in ORANGE and also in NEAR,

My fourth is in DRIVE but never in STEER,

My fifth is in GALLOP and always in TROT,

My sixth is in TOWN but isn't in NOT,

My whole is just like me but much harder to spot.

What am I? _____

At my house

My first is in FAMOUS and also in FAME,

My second's in PIPE but isn't in DRAIN,

My third is in NECK and also in NOSE,

My fourth is in ICE but isn't in FROZE,

My fifth is in CHANNEL and also in GROOVE,

My whole runs around the house but doesn't move.

What am I? _____

HINT Each line is a clue to a letter of the alphabet – put the letters in order to find the answer to the question.

Runaway Balloons

Rory, Niels, Charlotte, and Juanita are selling balloons as part of a fundraiser for a local animal hospital. During the rush to get started, the balloons have been mixed up and now the sellers aren't holding their own balloons. Can you help them find the right ones? With a line, match the definitions on each balloon to the word on one of the seller's T-shirts.

HINT Each seller should have four balloons.

Rory — bore

Niels — defect

Charlotte — address

Juanita — move

a formal speech

to be tedious

to touch

to reposition

to desert

a shortcoming

to drill

a lecture

to be dull

a dwelling

an imperfection

to burrow

to affect

to rearrange

to abandon

a location

The Daily Press

eThe Daily Press is having a contest. In some of this week's news headlines, they've used two words that mean the same thing. The first reader to find the pair of words in each headline wins a prize. Can you be the first to find them?

eeChallenging Puzzles

EMPTY FERRY SINKS! PASSENGERS WATCH FROM SHORE AS FERRY SUBMERGES

Triumphant musicians celebrate successful concert as crowds give standing ovation!

3–0 VICTORY SUPPORTS ENGLAND COACH'S CLAIM THAT ROBUST TRAINING PRODUCED A STRONG TEAM

Nimble hamster has lucky escape as agile ten-year-old climbs tree to its rescue

HARSH WORDS FROM EMPLOYEES AS STRICT BOSS SAYS NO TO CHRISTMAS PARTY

The secret to a long life is eating lots of chocolate, claims confidential report

The prize the newspaper is offering is shown below, but the letters are all mixed up. Work out what the lucky winner will get by unscrambling the letters.

iceman kitsect

— — — — — —   — — — — — —

ee(32)

Number Pyramids

Donna was meant to be making up some number pyramids but she was distracted and has left some incomplete. Can you finish them for her?

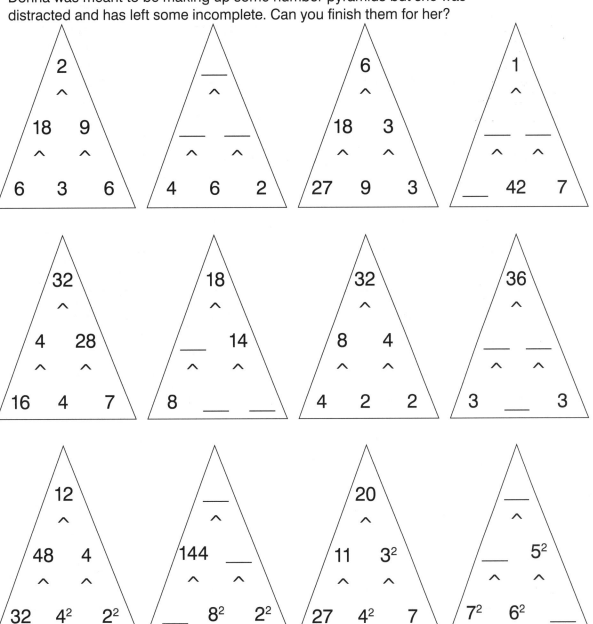

The Running Backwards Race

Oppositeville is having a race. Everything in Oppositeville is done backwards, including races! In this running race there are two teams: Team Back and Team Ward. The first team to reach the START line wins.

HINT As you go along, you may want to write the letter 'B' or 'W' above the stones.

The Rules

1   In order for each team member to take a step backwards, they must match one of the words on their team's flags with one of the words on the rocks behind them. The words on the team flags mean the opposite of a word in one of the two rows of stones.

2   No rock can be skipped. Each team must match a flag word with one of the words on the first two rocks, then one of the second pair of rocks, and so on.

The teams are ready so … On your marks … Get set … Go!

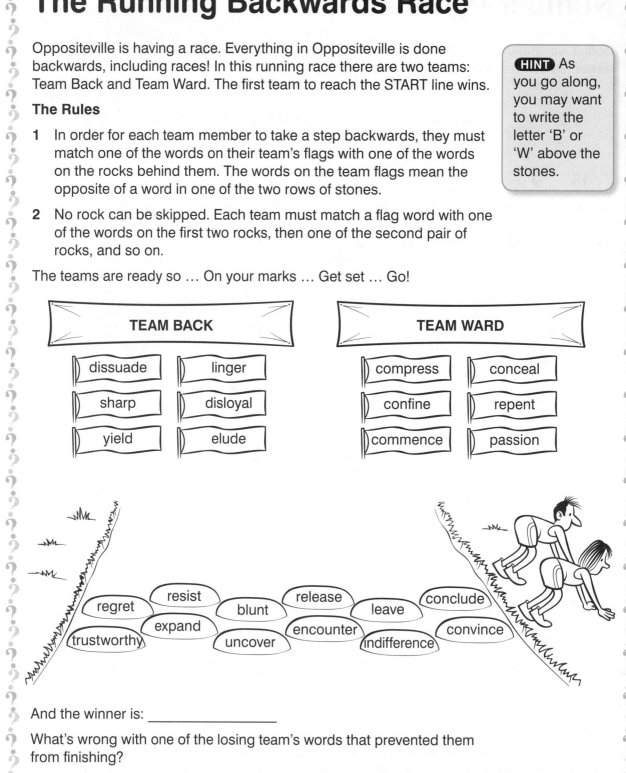

TEAM BACK

dissuade	linger
sharp	disloyal
yield	elude

TEAM WARD

compress	conceal
confine	repent
commence	passion

regret resist blunt release leave conclude
trustworthy expand uncover encounter indifference convince

And the winner is: _____

What's wrong with one of the losing team's words that prevented them from finishing?

_____

Where's My Bike?

Ollie's bike disappeared a few days ago so he decided to go to the police station for help. When he arrived, Officer Foyle asked him to write down the facts about the events of the last few days. Here is Ollie's account.

Midtown Police Report

Name: Ollie Wells   Age: 12 years

Subject: Missing bike

Facts:

- I have a red ten-speed bike.
- I rode my bike home from school on Friday and put it in the garage.
- I walked to my friend Matt's house on Saturday. Matt's mum drove us to swimming practice.
- On Sunday morning I went to the garage and found that my bike was missing.
- On Monday, I put up a poster in local shops about my missing bike.
- Later that day, my mate Jim told me that a bike had been found in Grenville Park.

After reading Ollie's report, Officer Foyle made one comment that must have been true. What do you think Officer Foyle said?

> **HINT** Some of the comments **might** be true, but only one is **definitely** true.

So, someone's stolen your bike.

So, you had to walk to school on Monday.

So, your bike was gone all weekend.

So, it was your bike that was found in the park.

So, you couldn't ride your bike on Sunday.

Four Peaks Challenge

Help Sir Monty meet the Four Peaks Challenge. To do this, he has to reach the top four of the highest mountain peaks in the world and plant one flag on each summit. Help Sir Monty succeed by adding one letter each time to the two-letter word given to create a new word. Each new word matches one of the clues.

Mount Everest

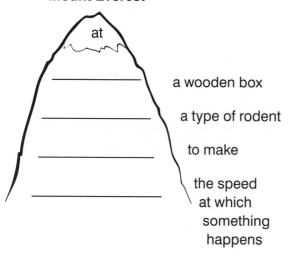

at

_____   a wooden box

_____   a type of rodent

_____   to make

_____   the speed at which something happens

> **HINT** Beware! The clues for each peak aren't in order.

K2

it

a large hole in the ground

_____

used for supporting a broken bone

_____

to forcibly eject from one's mouth

_____

to break into parts

_____

Kangchenjunga

an

precipitation   _____

a type of transportation   _____

to have moved faster than a walk   _____

nervous tension   _____

Lhotse

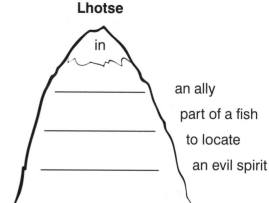

in

_____   an ally

_____   part of a fish

_____   to locate

_____   an evil spirit

_____

Painting by Numbers

Each of these paint colours is represented by a number. Can you work out which number stands for each individual colour?

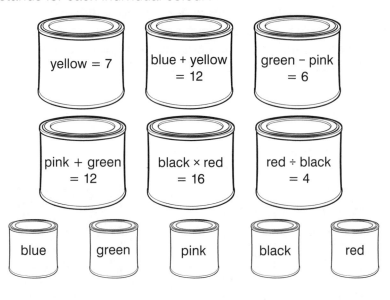

yellow = 7

blue + yellow = 12

green – pink = 6

pink + green = 12

black × red = 16

red ÷ black = 4

blue   green   pink   black   red

_____   _____   _____   _____   _____

The Playle sisters are painting their rooms. Can you work out which colour each girl has chosen?

Isabella $\dfrac{(\text{green} \times \text{blue}) - (\text{blue} \times \text{pink})}{(\text{blue} \times \text{black})} =$

Ella $\dfrac{(4 \times \text{red}) - \text{blue}}{\text{pink}^2} =$

Andrea $\dfrac{\left(\text{pink} \times \dfrac{\text{red}}{\text{black}} + \text{black}\right)}{\text{black}} =$

Martha $\dfrac{(\text{blue}^2 - \text{green})}{\text{black}} =$

Scrabble Scramble!

Aileen and Lawrie are playing a word game, taking it in turns to make a word from their letters and place it on the game board. Unfortunately, Molly, Aileen's spaniel, has knocked the board and several letters have scattered across the table. Can you help Aileen and Lawrie put the letters back in the correct places so that they can continue their game? Some clues to the words they made are given below the board.

men   **eat**   **hem**

her   **rap**

lip

1 a				2 d				3 e
p				i				c
				s				
		4 c				5 a		
						d		
l								s
				6 t				e
		s						
7 b	r					h	e	

tan   **oar**   **pea**

Clues

1 across: to alter or change
   down: to plead

2 across: to hang or loosely cover
   down: far away

3 to hide or overshadow

4 rough

5 to stick or hold fast

6 a subject or topic

7 to inhale and exhale

Let's Get Cooking!

Chef Pierre doesn't have time to complete all of the dishes for the busy lunchtime service in his restaurant, so he has asked you to finish some for him. He has managed to prepare five recipes for you to follow.

On each left-hand table you will find some word ingredients in measuring cups. Chef Pierre has mixed together some of the letters from these word ingredients to make the new word mixture in the bowl. You must follow each recipe to create a similar dish using the ingredients on the right-hand tables. Happy cooking!

1
charm   camel   elite   trays   teeth

2
slope   petal   talks   ankle   verve

3
spore   prose   repel   mains   recap

4
stove   table   blank   drive   flier

5
panel   neaten   eaten   label   saver

Pig Latin!

Here are some movie sayings that have been translated into Pig Latin (a made-up language). Can you work out what they say? The first one will give you a clue.

HINT Pay attention to vowels and consonants!

otay infinityyay andyay eyondbay!   To infinity and beyond!

1   **I'llyay etgay ouyay ymay rettypay – andyay ouryay ittlelay ogday ootay.**

_____

_____

2   **Ityay oesday otnay oday otay wellday onyay reamsday, arryHay, andyay orgetfay otay ivelay.**

_____

_____

Now, can you work out what these movie quotes would look like in Pig Latin?

3   **I'm not a puppet. I'm a real boy.**

_____

_____

4   **We have to do dogs' work. You're a pig. Your job is to stay here and eat your food.**

_____

_____

HINT There is one rule for words that start with a vowel and a different rule for words that start with a consonant.

Fussy Eaters!

One busy Tuesday lunchtime at Sanjay's Indian Restaurant, something unusual happened. Each customer only wanted varieties of word foods that were related in some way to each other. No one told the chef, so this meant that any unrelated foods had to be removed from each plate before they could be served to the customers. Sanjay put the unrelated foods on a separate table for the staff to have for their lunch. Which foods do you think Sanjay had to put aside from each order?

HINT The number of foods to be removed from each plate varies.

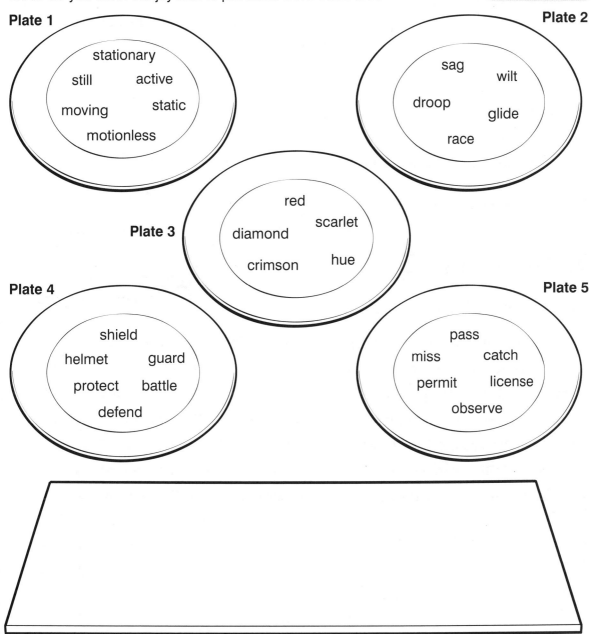

Plate 1
stationary
still   active
moving   static
motionless

Plate 2
sag   wilt
droop   glide
race

Plate 3
red
scarlet
diamond
crimson   hue

Plate 4
shield
helmet   guard
protect   battle
defend

Plate 5
pass
miss   catch
permit   license
observe

Riddle Time

HINT It may help to write out the alphabet.

Can you solve the riddles? Find the two letters that continue the pattern, then put the letters you've found together to solve the riddles.

CL is to DK as EJ is to ____ ____

LY is to NA as PC is to ____ ____

I grow when I eat but die when I drink.

What am I? _____

JK is to GN as DQ is to ____ ____

LT is to MU as NV is to ____ ____

HR is to GP as FN is to ____ ____

What gets wetter the more that it dries?

____ _____

RO is to UK as XG is to ____ ____

FY is to XQ as PI is to ____ ____

MN is to LO as JQ is to ____ ____

I have arms, legs and a back but never walk anywhere.

What am I? ____ _____

What Am I? 3

HINT Each line is a clue to a letter of the alphabet.

Solve the riddles to answer the questions.

My first is in PLUM and also in PEACH,

My second's in TRAIN but never in TEACH,

My third is in GOSH and also in GOLLY,

My fourth is in MOLLY but isn't in FOLLY,

My fifth is in PAIR as well as in TWIN,

My sixth is in FISH but isn't in FIN,

My seventh is in TICKET and also in TOKEN,

My whole which if spoken is also then broken.

What am I? _____

My first is in NOTE and not in LONE,

My second's in SEE but isn't in SHOWN,

My third is in GOLF and always in BALL,

My fourth is in CREEP but never in CRAWL,

My fifth is in PETER and also in PAN,

My sixth is in HIM but never in MAN,

My seventh is in HORSE and always in COW,

My eighth is in BRANCH but never in BOUGH,

My ninth is in SINGER and also in DANCER,

My whole asks no questions but demands an answer.

What am I? _____

Word Pairs Wordsearch

In this wordsearch there are 20 words that are made up of two smaller words. The words may be found in any direction (up, down, forwards, backwards or diagonally). When you've found a word, draw a circle around it. One has been found to get you started.

as	car	ram	page	prim	ever
cent	bar	go	the	green	ate
rest	row	tune	me	row	fur
ran	rain	for	do	ore	bat
sack	cast	fore	rest	main	he
nation	do	ring	tea	rust	mist

Word Match

The Red and Blue teams are about to have a match. Each player must pair up with a member of the other team, but they have to find each other first. Instead of wearing numbers, each player has a pair of words on their shirt. The words in each word pair are related in some way.

Help the players pair up correctly by connecting each red shirt with the correct blue shirt. The word pairs in the matching shirts will be related in the same way. The first pair of players have already found one another.

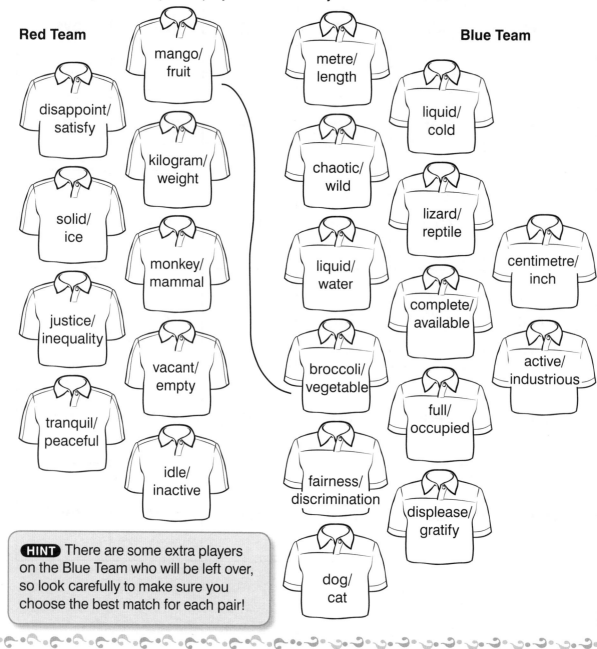

Red Team

mango/ fruit

disappoint/ satisfy

kilogram/ weight

solid/ ice

monkey/ mammal

justice/ inequality

vacant/ empty

tranquil/ peaceful

idle/ inactive

Blue Team

metre/ length

liquid/ cold

chaotic/ wild

lizard/ reptile

liquid/ water

centimetre/ inch

complete/ available

broccoli/ vegetable

active/ industrious

full/ occupied

fairness/ discrimination

displease/ gratify

dog/ cat

HINT There are some extra players on the Blue Team who will be left over, so look carefully to make sure you choose the best match for each pair!

While We're Away ...

Mum and Dad have gone away for the weekend and left the girls in charge! Of course, Mum and Dad have left some instructions for some things they want the girls to do while they're away. The notes are written in code; fortunately Mum and Dad have given them a starting point to work out the code for each note. Can you help the girls decipher their parents' notes?

HINT Each note has its own code. It may help if you write out the alphabet!

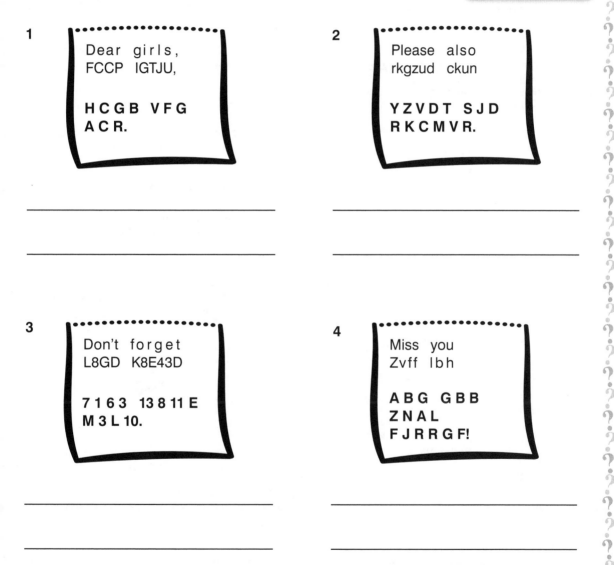

1

Dear girls,
FCCP IGTJU,

HCGB VFG
ACR.

_____

_____

2

Please also
rkgzud ckun

YZVDT SJD
RKCMVR.

_____

_____

3

Don't forget
L8GD K8E43D

7 1 6 3   13 8 11 E
M 3 L 10.

_____

_____

4

Miss you
Zvff lbh

ABG GBB
ZNAL
FJRRGF!

_____

_____

HINT Remember that to decode an encoded message, you'll have to reverse the way the code is made for the message to make sense – and vice versa!

Answers

Who's Right? B 25
Colette

Before and After B 8
2 fish   **3** cup   **4** pan   **5** paper   **6** pick   **7** end
8 life   **9** book   **10** man   **11** card   **12** ball

Sign Language B 24
A elf; fowl; wolf   **B** flower   **C** lo; of; or; ow; we; few; foe; for; fro; low; owe; owl; roe: row; woe; flew; flow; fore; lore; role; wore; lower

Hidden Creatures B 21
2 heart-th**rob in**vited   **3** tan**go at**   **4** magician**'s wan**d
5 Ja**cob ra**n   **6** n**ot ter**ribly   **7** flip**pant her**o
8 battles**hip po**unded   **9** wardro**be e**ven
10 **a pe**anut   The missing animal is an ape!

It's Your Go! B 23
Jack: [A♠]   Jill: [10♠]

Humpty Dumpty: [6♠] followed by [4♣]

Build the Wall B 5
weightless   **gift/here**   boring   stone   apartment   clever
light   present   **dull**   **rock**   **flat**   **bright**
ignite   **here/gift**   cloudy   sway   level   light

Fish Ponds B 4
1 glove, shoe   **2** imaginary, invented   **3** slip, trip
4 lesson, class   **5** tire, bore

Roll of the Dice B 26
Lucy: 10   Kate: 4   Nathan: 10   Ali: 12   Jean-Baptiste: 6
1 Ali   **2** Lucy and Nathan

At the Cinema B 25
Ian, Mia, Lucy, Georgia, Tom, Reese, Ahmed

Dear Planet Earth B 24
We come in peace. We want only one thing – to come and watch an Earthling cricket match.
Zpv bsf nptu xfmdpnf, gsjfoet.

World of Word Burgers B 13
01 ash, flash   **02** win, twine   **03** in, tint   **04** art, party
05 rim, grime   **06** pan, panel   **07** air, flair

Ship Ahoy!

Ship 1: $11 + 8 - 2$
Ship 3: $3 \times 2 + 5$
Ship 2: $\frac{9}{3} \times 4$
Ship 4: $6 \times 2 + 3$
Ship 3: $10 \times 0 + 11$

What Am I? 1 B 25
Pass the Tissues: cold; Up and down: stairs

Here and There B 18 B 24
1 Herts   **2** shireP   **3** Nods   **4** This   **5** Late
west; south; north; east; Truro

Is Something Out There? B 22
Line 1: **ora**nge   Line 2: cl**aim**ed   Line 3: b**all**oons
Line 4: govern**men**t, **Ear**th   Line 5: be**for**e, to**war**ds
Line 7: el**even**, ali**en**s   Line 9: app**ear**ed

Your Turn! B 23
Game 1: [J♥]   Game 2: [7♠] [7♥]

Game 3: [4♣] [J♣]

Word Soup B 8
bargain; canon; combat; courtyard; dome; notice; passage; ransack; tablet; target

Get Me Out of Here! B 10
wis**health**amme**radio**per**ankle**as**tomat**
octopusee**saw**
A hot shower!

True or False? B 25
Tigs is indoors at night.

Terrible Toddlers! B 23
Top shelf: Ducklings Waddle   Finn's Unicorn
Second shelf: Meet Owen   Prince Richard

Brain Benders

A red **B** Martin – three-meat special: pepperoni, ham and sausage; Anna – tomato, basil and olive; Mandy – pineapple, basil, tomato and sausage; Manuel – red pepper, tomato and mushroom; Rolf – ham and onion; Mr Wilson – pepperoni

Find the Missing Letters

Z 2 T 3 X

It's a Mystery!

stormy / endure / drifting / dangerous / convict / insane / roused / back / wearily / seized / remembered

House!

Call 1: 25 *Call 2:* 9 *Call 3:* 7 *Call 4:* 15 *Call 5:* 2 *Call 6:* 12
Congratulations! <u>Jules</u> won the jackpot!

Alice in Wonderland

old / affectionately / pleasant / perhaps / savage / hopeful / sour / stingy / forgotten / startled

It's a Lot of Hot Air!

Balloon 1: The words mean the same.
suspend/hang; banish/remove; cunning/crafty
Balloon 2: The words mean the opposite.
unite/divide; peril/safety; release/hold
Balloon 3: The first word represents a part or element of the second word.
handle/hammer; pip/orange; mother/family
Balloon 4: The second word represents the type of category to which the first word belongs.
encyclopaedia/book; cheddar/cheese; orang-utan/mammal

Can You Crack the Code?

The treasure chest can be found next to the coconut tree, under the black rock. But beware, the chest may not be the only thing hidden under the rock!
6 2 22 26 2 26, 24 26 11 7 26 18 13 8 14 18 7 19.
1 12 6 13 23 7 19 22 9 12 24 16, 25 6 7 18 7
5 12 12 16 8 15 18 16 22 2 12 6 9 12 15 23
2 13 22 14 2 11 22 20 15 22 20 20 12 7 7 19 22 9 22
1 18 9 8 7!

My Shopping Basket

beans: 92635 *mango:* 4631x *juice:* 8a7b2
dates: y6z25
nuts; onions; cocoa; tomatoes

What Am I? 2

Look, quick!: shadow At my house: fence

Runaway Balloons

bory: to be dull, to be tedious, to drill, to burrow;

Niels: to abandon, to desert, a shortcoming, an imperfection; Charlotte: a lecture, a formal speech, a dwelling, a location; Juanita: to touch, to affect, to reposition, to rearrange

The Daily Press

sinks, submerges; triumphant, successful; robust, strong; nimble, agile; harsh, strict; secret, confidential
cinema tickets

Number Pyramids

	3			1			18	
24	8		6	6		4	14	
4	6	2	48	42	7	8	2	7

	36			9			38	
6	6		144	16		13	5^2	
3	2	3	80	8^2	2^2	7^2	6^2	11

The Running Backwards Race

Team Back: (convince/dissuade; leave/linger; encounter/elude; blunt/sharp; resist/yield; trustworthy/disloyal)
Team Ward: (conclude/commence; release/confine; uncover/conceal; expand/compress)
Team Back is the winning team because Team Ward's last word, 'regret', means the same as, and not the opposite of, 'repent'.

Where's My Bike?

So, you couldn't ride your bike on Sunday.

Four Peaks Challenge

Mount Everest	K2	Kangchenjunga
at	it	an
rat	pit	ran
rate	spit	rain
crate	split	train
create	splint	strain

Lhotse
in
fin
find
fiend
friend

Painting by Numbers

blue – 5; green – 9; pink – 3; black – 2; red – 8
Isabella – pink; Ella – pink; Martha – red; Andrea – yellow

Scrabble Scramble!

1 across: amend; down: appeal **2** across: drape; down: distant **3** eclipse **4** coarse **5** adhere **6** theme **7** breathe

Let's Get Cooking!

1 taste **2** lever **3** crime **4** rifle **5** beaver

Pig Latin! B 24

1 I'll get you my pretty – and your little dog too.
2 It does not do to dwell on dreams, Harry, and forget to live.
3 I'myay otnay ayay uppetpay. I'myay ayay ealray oybay.
4 eWay avehay otay oday ogsday' orkway. ou'reYay ayay igpay. ouryay objay isyay otay taysay erehay andyay eatyay ouryay oodfay.

Fussy Eaters! B 4

Plate 1: active, moving; Plate 2: glide, race;
Plate 3: diamond, hue; Plate 4: helmet, battle;
Plate 5: miss, catch, observe

Riddle Time B 23

FI / RE: fire; AT / OW / EL: a towel; AC / HA / IR: a chair

What Am I? 3 B 25

promise; telephone

Word Pairs Wordsearch B 8

as	car	ram	page	prim	ever
cent	bar	go	the	green	ate
rest	row	tune	me	row	fur
ran	rain	for	do	ore	bat
sack	cast	fore	rest	main	he
nation	do	ring	tea	rust	mist

ascent; barrow; bathe; cargo; domain; dome; donation; evergreen; forecast; fortune; furore; furrow; mistrust; primate; rampage; ransack; restore; restrain; tearing; theme

Word Match B 15

disappoint / satisfy – displease / gratify;
kilogram / weight – metre / length;
solid / ice – liquid / water;
monkey / mammal – lizard / reptile;
justice / inequality – fairness / discrimination;
vacant / empty – occupied / full;
tranquil / peaceful – chaotic / wild;
idle / inactive – active / industrious

While We're Away … B 24

1 Feed the cat.   **2** Water the plants.
3 Make your beds.   **4** Not too many sweets!